Johnston-Hale
PUBLICATIONS

Queen
a Collection of Poems

Joanne Boyle

Illustrated by
Naomi Hands-Smith

Produced by
Johnston-Hale Publications
in the United Kingdom
2022

www.johnston-hale.co.uk

Issue 1

Author Joanne Boyle
Illustrator Naomi Hands-Smith

Johnston-Hale
PUBLICATIONS

The named contributors of this book have asserted their rights under the Copyright, Designs and Patents Act of 1988 to be identified as the authors and illustrators of this work.

A note from the Poet:

Upon hearing about the death of our beloved Queen, I like everyone else, felt such a loss and a great sadness.

This inspired me to write the poem 'Queen'. The response I received from all over the world, went on to inspire me to go on to write this short book of poems.

I hope it brings comfort to many.

Joanne xx

Dedicated to our Queen

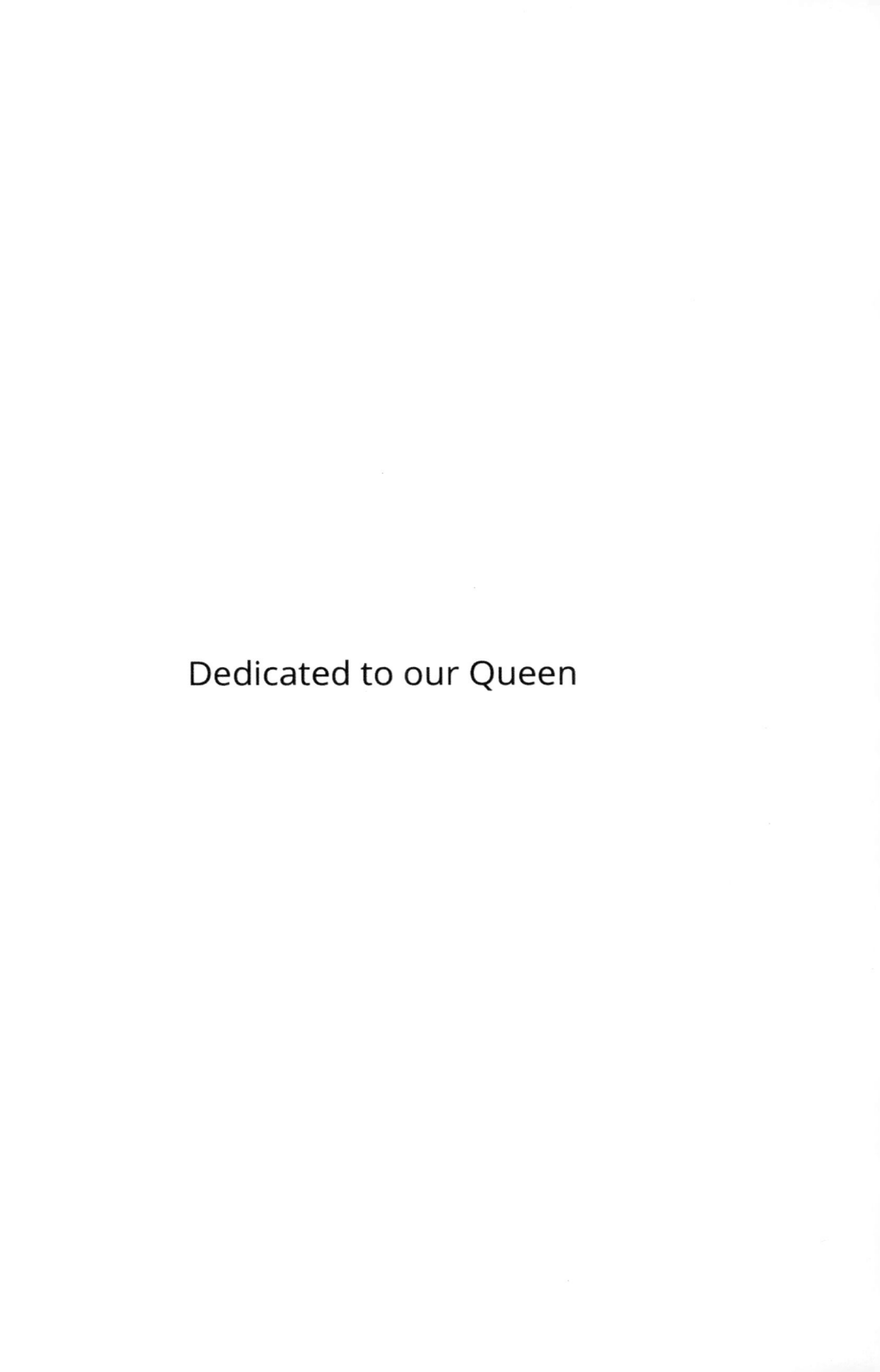

Queen

Philip came to me today
and said "It's time to go".
I looked at him and smiled,
then whispered, "Yes I know".

I turned and looked behind me,
and saw myself asleep.
All the family were around me,
and I could hear them weep.

I gently touched each shoulder
with Philip by my side.
I turned from them and walked away
with my angel husband as a guide.

Philip held my hand,
as he led me on the way.
To a world where kings and queens
are monarchs every day.

Still I have a crown to wear,
a halo known by some.
The difference is up here
they are worn by everyone.

I felt a sense of peace,
my reign had seen its end.
70 years I'd served my Country,
as the people's dearest friend.

Thank you for the years,
for all your time and love.
Now I am one of two again,
in our palace up above.

Grandchildren

Come sit with me children,
I have a story for you to hear.
I know you are still young,
so I want to make this clear.

I grew up in a time,
one you won't remember.
A time we lost our Queen,
on the 8th day of September.

The Queen was also a Grandma,
like I and many others.
She was a great inspiration,
to all of us Mothers.

You are now part of a new era,
of which you will greet a king.
Please try to read the History,
and hold on to everything.

Tradition is important,
and will help you both to grow..
By embracing past events,
your knowledge will then flow.

By embracing life's history,
it will help you on your way,
but for now keep on having fun,
and living for today.

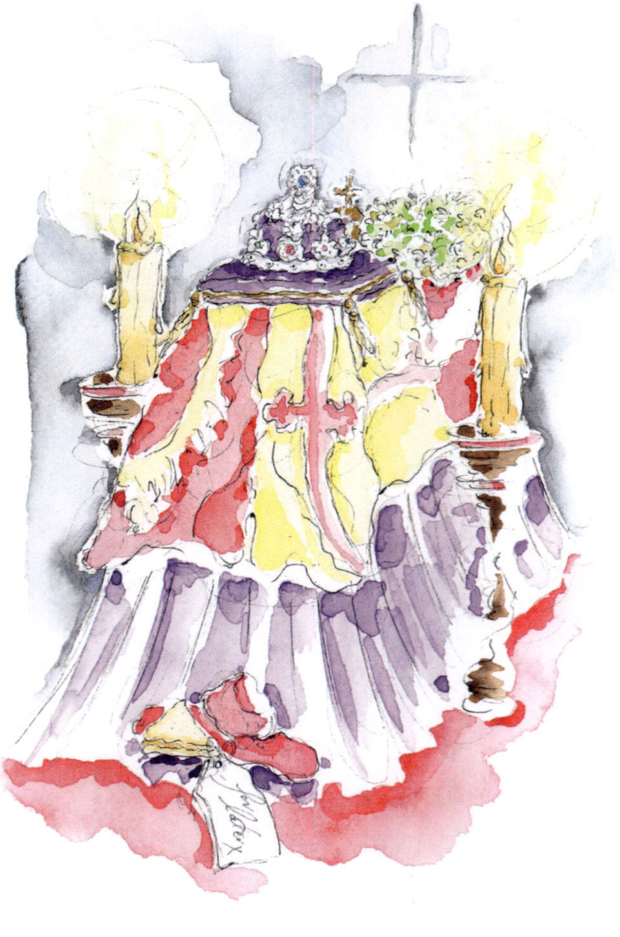

Journey Home

This is not my final Journey,
just the beginning of something new.
It is the end of an era,
but I still have work to do.

I heard there were some Angels,
that were looking for a Queen.
Who needed some inspiration,
from a past time that has been.

God knew that I was ready,
He knew the King was too.
So he gave me a new role,
and took me to pastures new.

He knew the King would reign,
and become the people's King.
And the new national Anthem,
would be the song that we now sing.

The words will echo up above,
'God Save our Gracious King'.
I shall be proudly watching,
as my son's new journey shall begin.

My Mind's Eye

I sit upon my sofa, lost amongst the crowd.
There is an eery silence, but my heart is beating loud.

Millions of people travelled, to pay their final respects.
I have a first hand view, from my mind's effects.

I smell the pretty flowers; I am lost amidst the scent.
I am surrounded by the people's love, because in my mind I went.

The procession walked right past me, from my sofa I'm in awe.
How privileged I am, for everything I saw.

Our Queen she looked so beautiful, with her crown upon her head.
A flag of representation, warmed her in her bed.

There was an aid for her awakening, a sceptre some will say.
To me it was a crutch, to help her on her way.

I felt each family's heartache, from sitting in my chair.
I reached and hugged each one of them, as I would if I was there.

I shed a silent tear, a drop became a fall.
I am full of admiration, for a country that stands tall.

I listen to the words, the ones so proudly read.
I type them in my heart, as I hear them loudly said.

I feel the glow around me, to be part of history.
As I watch on from my sofa...My Imagination...and me.

Paddington Bear

Dear Paddington bear,
my friend with his marmalade jam.
The one who liked to come for tea,
and addressed me as his Ma am.

I am going to miss you,
but not your sticky fingers!
You gave many laughs down there,
which here in heaven linger.

I am glad you came to visit,
on my jubilee...
We left all that watched our video,
with a happy memory.

I will tell the angel children,
of all the stories that we shared.
About how little Paddington bear,
stopped people feeling scared.

I shall paint them all a picture,
of a bear with his red hat;
Sitting at a table,
where the Queen was also sat.

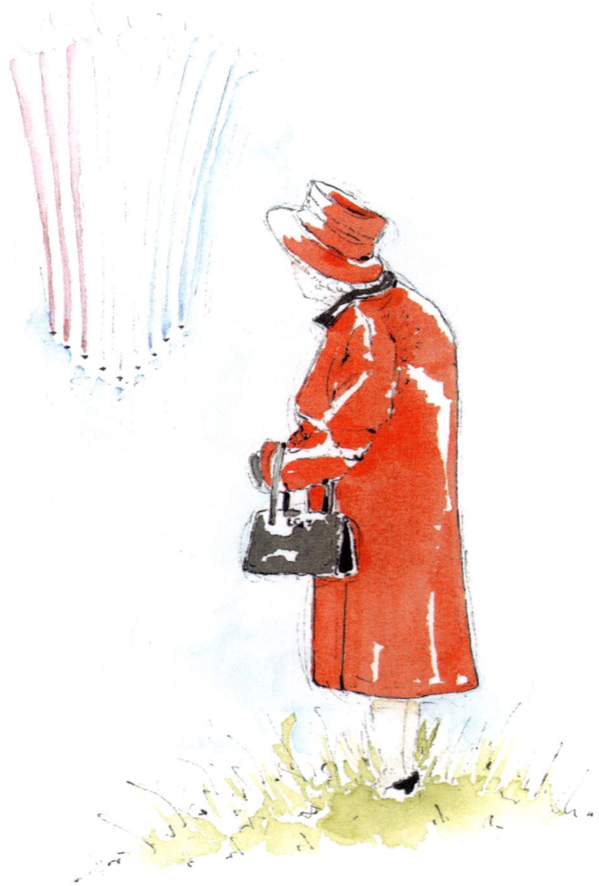

Serenity

Farewell the people's Queen;
you were the Country's friend.
A Mother and a GrandMother,
your legacy shall not end.

Hello the Future King;
just be your Mother's son.
Be the country's friend,
of hearts your dear Ma am won.

Farewell to the Queen's reign,
one we shall remember.
A time we all stood still;
on the 8th of September.

Hello to each new moment,
to the history we are yet to make.
To the memories we all hold,
and a past we will not forsake.

Farewell to yesterday,
to a life you made from love.
Hello to serenity,
with your Philip up above.

Sovereign

I received a pass from Heaven, saying there was somewhere to attend.
It was then I saw a beautiful car, coming around the bend.

I turned and looked at Philip. I asked if he could come too.
After all he was a part of me, a part of my reign too.

God granted us this wish and opened the pearly gate.
We walked down the golden staircase, to where the carriages await.

The streets were full of people, though we expected nothing less.
All of them looked on, to see the final address.

The silence made it extra special. That was something new.
Young and old had travelled, and to those I say 'Thank you'.

The military marched exquisitely, not one step out of place.
My Family did me proud, as they walked with so much grace.

Every word that people spoke, heard with our own ears.
So many cotton handkerchiefs, to catch so many tears.

I now live on in your King, but I will never leave his side.
I will be watching from the sky, a Mother filled with pride.

Seated

Do not look at me with sorrow,
simply because I sit alone.
It is a choice I chose to make,
to compose the shivers from my bone.

Do not look at me with pity,
as it is what I chose to do.
It was Philip's place to be,
which I wanted to show to you.

My world of love is shattered,
and my heart is broke in two,
but as the people's Queen
I still have a job to do.

Thank you all for your kind words,
as I laid my Husband to rest.
I had 73 wonderful years,
being married to the best.

So do not look at me with sorrow,
for a choice that I did make.
I chose to sit alone,
for my country's sake.

The seat beside me was my Husband's;
It was not an empty space.
His presence was beside me,
you just couldn't see his face.

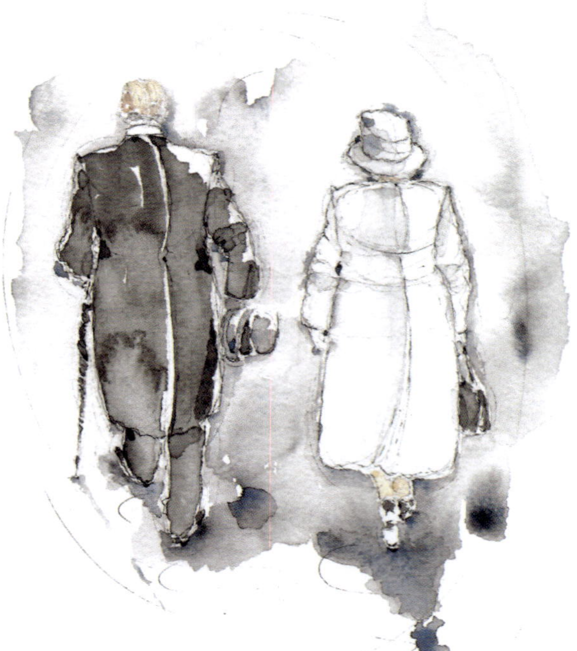

Take me Home

Take me Home,
to where I lay.
To where the tunes,
of bagpipes play.

Take me home,
to where memories dance.
Where flowers bloom,
at every chance.

Take me home,
to where peace resides.
In fields of green
and dewdrops glide.

Take me home,
to where I sleep.
Inside your heart,
where I will keep.

The Queen's Nightdress

Wrapped in my last nightdress,
I lay in a silent dream.
Not a whisper can be heard,
not a breath to be seen.

I feel so warm and loved,
guarded by my own.
My Daughter and my boys,
oh what courage you have shown.

The friends that came to love me,
all stand there tall and proud.
I watch from heaven's doorway,
to praise this amazing crowd.

Surrounded by so much love,
though silence does prevail.
I am the Queen of angels,
and on a cloud I shall now sail.

The colours of my country,
a blanket to warm my soul.
A lifetime full of memories,
to keep my spirit whole.

The crown upon my head,
compliments my nightdress.
I sleep with ever lasting peace,
and to all:
Goodnight and Godbless.

The Day After

The world woke up in mourning,
a period of 10 days for us to share.
70 years of memories,
and a country in despair.

Flags were raised half-mast,
In regard of the highest respect.
The TV channels were full of stories,
of events that were correct.

A lady wrote a poem,
to paint a picture of comfort and peace.
She spoke of Philip's arrival,
and of a reign's release.

The world rejoiced in reels,
of past times been and gone.
Memories of a younger life,
from a Queen we'd had for so long.

People then made arrangements,
to go and lay flowers at Green Park.
People lined up to wait,
from morning until dark.

Our Queen had sadly left us,
but her spirit will never die.
She just left her body sleeping,
whilst she floated to the sky.

The Traveller's Respect

People trevelled from miles around,
to place their gifts upon the ground.
Messages written from the heart,
sympathy cards for Your depart.

Gifts of bears that wore red hats,
Cuddly toys left on mats.
Poems and cards with meaningful words,
from many countries to show their hurt.

Nationalities joined together as one.
It didn't matter that the queues were long.
Children were silent in their play.
Even though they hadn't slept all day.

People cried openly,
and hugs were given freely.
No one pushed to get any closer.
All respected each others composure.

A sense of loss and love within,
a warming glow to ones own skin.
A day to remember and make you proud,
If you travelled to be in this crowd.

Two Queens
Two Mothers

I was just a girl,
when you took the Throne.
The one thing we have in common,
is the years that we have grown.

The History of time,
has been shared with me and you.
We are worlds apart,
but I went through it all too.

I watched you have your children,
before I had my own.
I've seen beneath your eyes,
the things that were not shown.

I heard when you had troubles;
It happens to us all.
But as the people's Queen,
you weren't allowed to fall.

I am also someone's Queen.
There are so many of us around.
Being Mothers together,
puts us on common ground.

Heaven's "Ma ams"

I got a special delivery today
hand given from the Queen.
She told me how you'd warmed a nation,
with a poem that she had seen.

From one mother to another,
we spoke about our kin.
I told her all about you,
how you blossom from within.

It is then we opened up the clouds,
so I could show her who you are.
I said "That's my girl down there,
I knew that she'd go far".

At this point you looked up into the sky,
like you knew we were there.
I sensed a sense of anguish,
a mother is always aware.

I blew you down a loving kiss,
and you placed your hand upon your cheek.
It is then I heard you sigh...
I know you do that when you're weak.

Queen Elizabeth said to tell you,
your poems have spread much love.
You have made two mothers very proud,
here in the heavens up above.

Paddington and the Jubilee Tea

I was born a baby
just like all of you.
I loved a doll - a teddy bear,
and would have loved Paddington too.

So when I was politely asked
if he could come for tea,
to share a marmalade sandwich
on behalf of my jubilee...

Well how could I resist?
The bear from my children's days.
He brought adventure to their lives,
with his clumsy ways.

So as we shared a teapot,
or more like - he drank it all!
I watched on in amusement,
because he was so small!

We shared a love of marmalade,
he hid it in his hat!
Mine was in my bag,
beside where I was sat.

My Younger Self

I was in fact in Kenya,
on that awful day.
When I heard the dreadful news,
that my father passed away.

Inside I felt so torn,
like someone had ripped out my heart.
I had to do what was expected,
what I'd been taught right from the start.

The years that followed were dutiful,
but with Prince Philip by my side,
I had a job to do,
and I had to do it with pride.

My Father had taught me well.
He had prepared me for this day.
Yet nothing could have prepared me,
for the fact he went away.

Silently I cried,
but to the world I seemed so strong.
One day I was touring the Commonwealth,
the next my Pa had gone.

The Corgis

The corgis move from room to room,
to see if I am there.
They gather at the footrest,
of my favourite chair.

Then they bark and get excited,
and the staff wonder just what for?
My precious corgis know I'm there,
they see me at the door.

I bend and whisper to them "Hush",
as I gently stroke their fur.
Then I see our Willow,
appear on the stair.

Suddenly the room was full,
with all my furry friends!
And heaven opened up it's stairway,
for us all to ascend.

King Charles

I still recall the first time that I held you,
and sat you on my knee.
You were my first born Son,
future king of our Country.

You brought laughter to our days
to both your father and I.
We loved our private moments,
away from the public eye.

I have watched you from my doorway,
this new Kingdom I call home.
I have wiped your silent tears,
when you have been alone.

You were born to be a King,
and I know you will do it well.
Please keep me alive in memories
and in the stories that you tell.

You are your mothers son.
Wear your title with pride.
And whenever you feel you need me,
then call me from inside.

Winston

For one last time I rode you,
did you feel me on your back?
The wind blew in my face,
as we went around the track.

It brought back many memories,
some good and some quite sad.
Riding on my racehorses,
were some of the best times that I had.

It was only fitting that you came,
for there was no horse like you.
To ride me to my final place,
knowing my father was there too.

The trooping of the colours,
just wouldn't have been the same.
if I had rode any other horse,
that did not have your name.

The End

Johnston-Hale
PUBLICATIONS

If you would like to publish your own book or poetry collection, just write to us at celia@copelia.co.uk with your submission or visit www.johnston-hale.co.uk

Printed in Great Britain
by Amazon